What is mindfulness?

Mindfulness is a powerful tool that can greatly benefit your child's emotional and mental well-being. By teaching children to be mindful, we help them develop important skills that will support them throughout their lives.

In each book your child will learn a new mindfulness technique.

In this book they learn to notice their surroundings in greater detail by using their 5 senses.

Acknowledgements

Special thanks to the pupils of Hilden Oaks Preparatory School for their beautiful illustrations, bringing Ziggy and Zen's adventures to life with creativity and joy.

I also want to thank my daughter Rhianna for encouraging me to write this book and for her role in bringing it to life.

Ziggy and Zen are best friends but they are very different.

Ziggy races through life without ever stopping to notice anything.

Zen is always present in the moment, taking everything in.

Although they go to the same places, they experience things very differently.

Ziggy and Zen are on holiday and today they are going to to the hotel pool for a swim.

As soon as they arrive, Ziggy throws his bag down on a chair, kicks off his shoes and immediately jumps into the pool, making a huge

SPLASH!

Somebody nearby is reading a book - her book gets wet from the splash, but Ziggy doesn't even notice.

Zen puts his bag on a chair and takes a moment to close his eyes and breathe in deeply, feeling the warmth of the sun on his face; he feels grateful to be here on his holiday.

Ziggy swims rapidly around the pool a couple of times, almost crashing into other swimmers because his head is in the water and he doesn't notice they are there.

Zen takes off his shoes and is surprised to notice how hot the ground is as he walks towards the pool. He enjoys the warmth of the tiles on his toes.

Zen stops at the edge of the pool and is mesmerised by the glistening of the sun reflecting on the water's surface. He thinks it looks like tiny stars in the water. It's the most magical thing he's ever seen.

He notices the ripples in the water coming over the swimming pool steps - gently at first and then bigger as Ziggy splashes past him.

As Zen takes his first steps into the pool, he notices the difference in heat from the hot floor to the cool, refreshing water.

He slowly walks down the steps, getting deeper into the water, enjoying the cold, tingly sensations on his body - first on his feet, then his ankles, then his legs and gradually all the way up to his tummy.

Ziggy has been around the pool twice and is now bored of swimming!

He gets out of the pool, sits on his chair and gets out his video game to play

Zen is still enjoying his swim, watching how the water ripples as his arms push through with every stroke.

He notices the smell of chlorine in the pool and smiles to himself as it reminds him of learning to swim when he was small.

He remembers his red rubber ring and how he used to be scared of the water.

Zen can hear sounds of other people on holiday, laughing and chatting - some in different languages. They all seem to be having fun and it makes Zen feel happy.

He stops swimming, looks down to the bottom of the pool and notices how it looks as though his feet are not connected to his legs - the water has distorted his view!

Zen chuckles and starts to play with the water. First he makes gentle waves so that he can no longer see his feet at all, then he counts how many seconds it takes to settle again.

Just then, Ziggy calls over to him. Ziggy is bored playing 'Chickens in Space' because it is hard to see the screen in the sunshine.

He is fed up and doesn't know what to do next.

 Zen suggests they play a different game. They can play 'Chickens in Space' any time, but Zen wants Ziggy to notice his surroundings here on holiday.

He asks Ziggy to find:

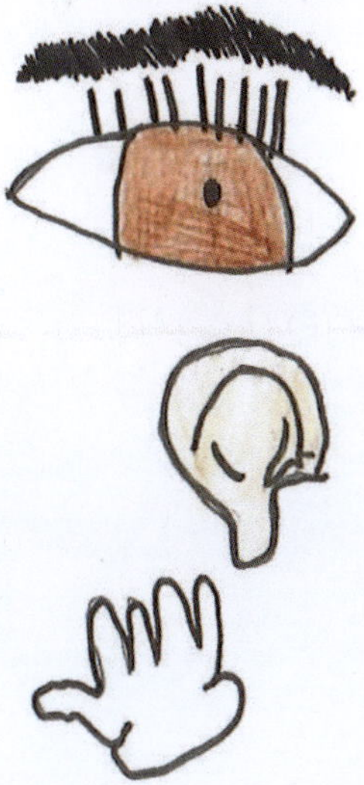

- **3** things he can **see**

- **3** things he can **hear**

- **2** things he can **feel**

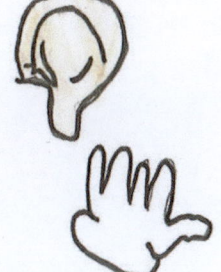

- **1** thing he can **smell**

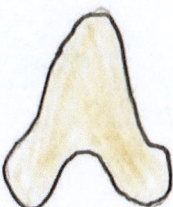

Ziggy can see:
- the pool,
- the sky,
- the hotel.

Zen can see:
- the sunlight shimmering on the water,
- the lizard hiding in the shade of the palm tree,
- the patterns on the tiles by the side of the pool.

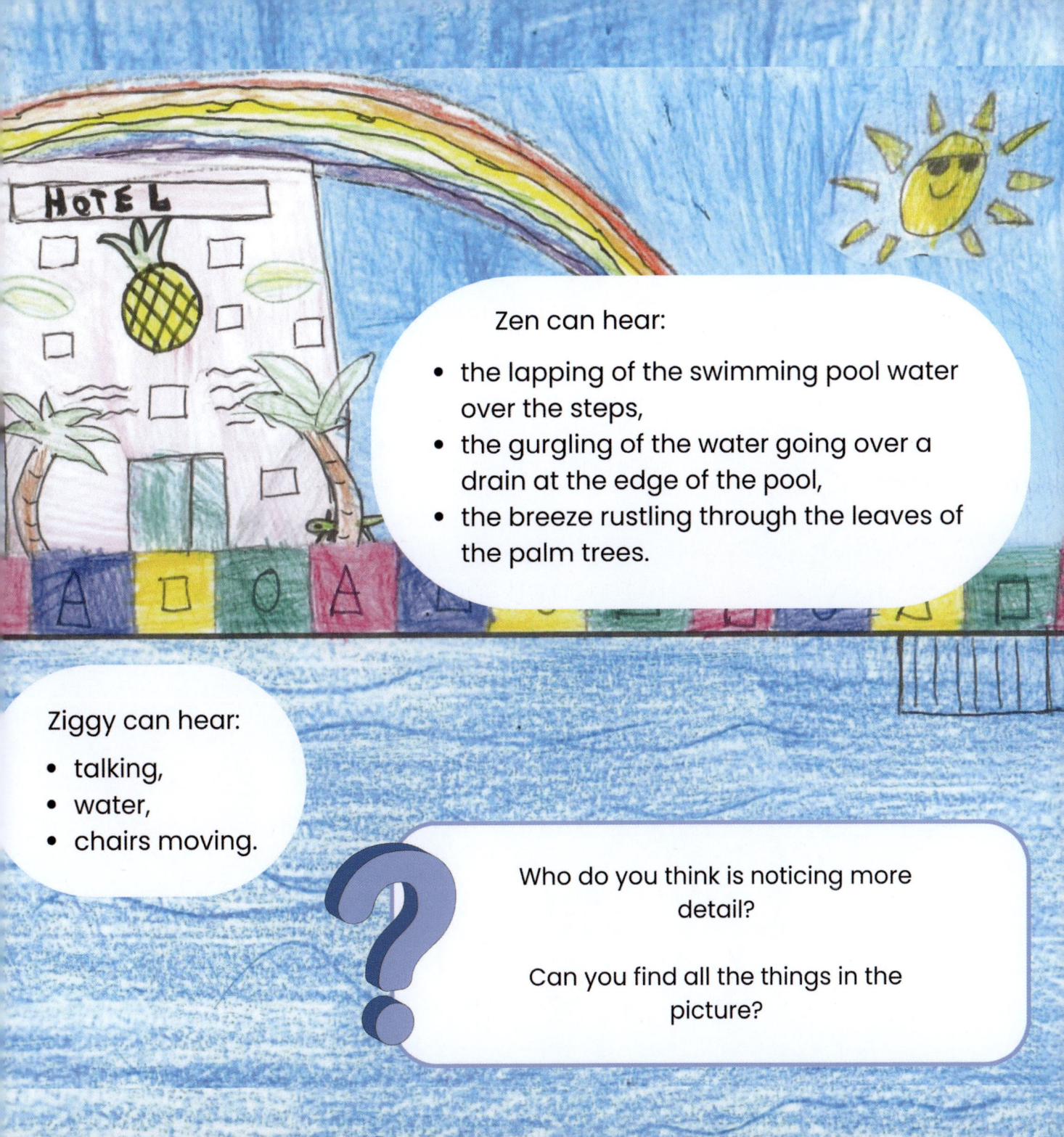

Ziggy can feel:
- his chair,
- his video game console.

Zen can feel:
- the droplets of water running down his body as the sun gently dries him,
- the warm breeze on his face.

Ziggy can smell:
- food cooking in the hotel restaurant.

Zen can smell:
- the smell of the fabric conditioner on his towel which reminds him of home.

Who do you think is more present in the moment?

Why?

After the senses game, Ziggy wants to leave the pool, so the two friends pack their things into their bags and head back to their hotel rooms.

Ziggy rushes straight back to his room. He goes so quickly, with his head down, that he doesn't even notice the poster!

Zen walks mindfully back to his room. On the way, he listens to the squelchy sound of his wet feet in his flipflops and feels the difference in temperature as he moves out of the sun into the shade.

He notices how the plants look different to the ones back home - some are spiky, some have different types of flowers on them, but Zen thinks the best one is the one with the enormous leaves.

Which plant do you like best? Why?

Finally, the friends get back to their hotel rooms, still wet from the pool.

Ziggy shivers and dries himself as quickly as possible to get back to playing 'Chickens in Space'. He doesn't like being wet and doesn't think he will bother to go swimming again on this holiday.

Zen closes his door and wraps his towel around his body tightly. He feels the warmth and softness of the towel on his skin.

Zen takes a in a deep breath and once again smells the fabric conditioner on the towel; it smells of home and reminds him how his Mum packed the towel for him in his suitcase. Zen smiles.

He feels as though the towel is giving him a big hug from his Mum which makes him feel happy and contented.

Zen is enjoying his holiday and feels very grateful to be here.

 Who do you think is having the best time on holiday? Ziggy or Zen?

Who have you been like today?

Are you like Ziggy rushing around without stopping to notice anything, or are you like Zen who is always present in the moment?

Drawing activity

Try playing Zen's game - look around you right now and draw 3 things you can see, 3 things you can hear, 2 things you can feel and 1 thing you can smell.

Ziggy or Zen activity

Tomorrow they are going to the beach. Who do you think is more likely to do these things?

Circle the character to show your answer.

 Gets cross when his sandcastle collapses.

 Notices the different shapes of shells.

 Breathes in and out in time with the waves on the shore.

 Runs to dive into the sea without looking and steps on a crab.

Pool activity

Next time you are at an outdoor pool, see if you can be like Zen and look out for these 8 things:

- [ ] Can you see the sun shimmering on the water?
- [ ] Can you see the water rippling over the steps so that the steps look like they are moving?
- [ ] Can you hear the sound of the water gurgling down the drain?
- [ ] Can you hear people speaking in different languages?
- [ ] Can you feel the breeze? Is it warm or cool?
- [ ] Can you feel the temperature of the floor? Is it hot or cold?
- [ ] Can you see any unusual or different plants?
- [ ] Can you feel the towel against your skin? How does it feel?

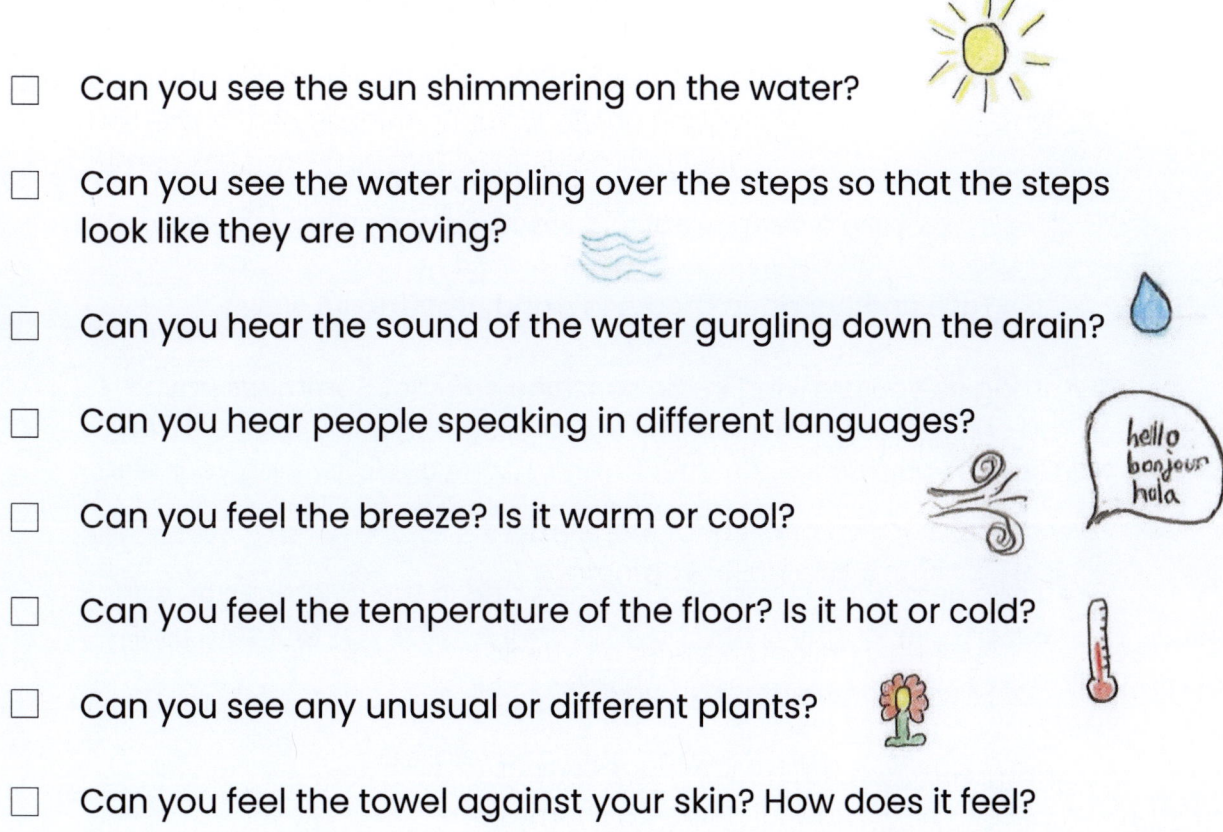

Guided meditation activity

Ask your child to lay on their backs in a comfortable space and close their eyes.

Put on some calming music quietly in the background and read the following guided meditation in a gentle voice.

Close your eyes, be as still as possible, and take a deep breath in. Breathe out slowly.

Take another deep breath in......and breathe out slowly.

Imagine you are lying in the sunshine on a hot Summer's day. You can feel the warmth of the sun on your face. You can feel the warmth on your arms.......on your tummy......on your legs.......on your feet. You feel calm and relaxed.

You can hear birds singing in the trees, and in the distance you can hear people laughing and having fun; it makes you feel safe and happy.

You are calm, safe and relaxed.

You can feel the soft cushion of the chair or blanket that you are lying on. Sink in deeper to the cushions.......Your whole body is relaxed and comfortable. There is no need to move and nothing to do. Just relax.

You are calm, safe and relaxed.

You can smell the wonderful scent of the flowers and the freshly cut grass. A delicious smell of your favourite meal being cooked is coming from the kitchen and you breathe in deeply to absorb the smell.

You are calm, safe and relaxed.

Take another big deep breath in and out, feeling grateful to be here in the sunshine. Think of all the happy times you have had in the sunshine and feel warm inside as the sun heats your body.

You are calm, safe and relaxed.

Lay there for as long as you like with this contented feeling and warmness inside.

Take this contented feeling with you in whatever you do for the rest of the day.

Remember you can return to this imaginary Summer's day, with its warm and relaxed feeling, whenever you like - just by closing your eyes!

Now when you are ready, open your eyes and bring your attention back into the room.

About the author

Wendy has been a primary school teacher since 1993, guiding and inspiring children aged 5-11 in both state and independent schools. With over 10 years experience as a mindfulness coach, she combines her love for teaching with mindfulness techniques, helping children cultivate calm and concentration in their daily routines.

Living in the beautiful county of Kent with her husband and two daughters, Wendy loves spending time with her family and walking in the countryside.

Wendy believes that every child can benefit from mindfulness, and she hopes her books will help them be more present in the moment, leading to a happier, more mindful life.

Meet the illustrators

Printed in Great Britain
by Amazon